Ducks

Illustrated by Henri Galeron
Created by Gallimard Jeunesse
and Jean-Philippe Chabot

MOONLIGHT PUBLISHING / FIRST DISCOVERY

Ducks fly and swim, they paddle and dive.
Ducks like water and wide open spaces.
Some ducks are wild,
others live close to people.

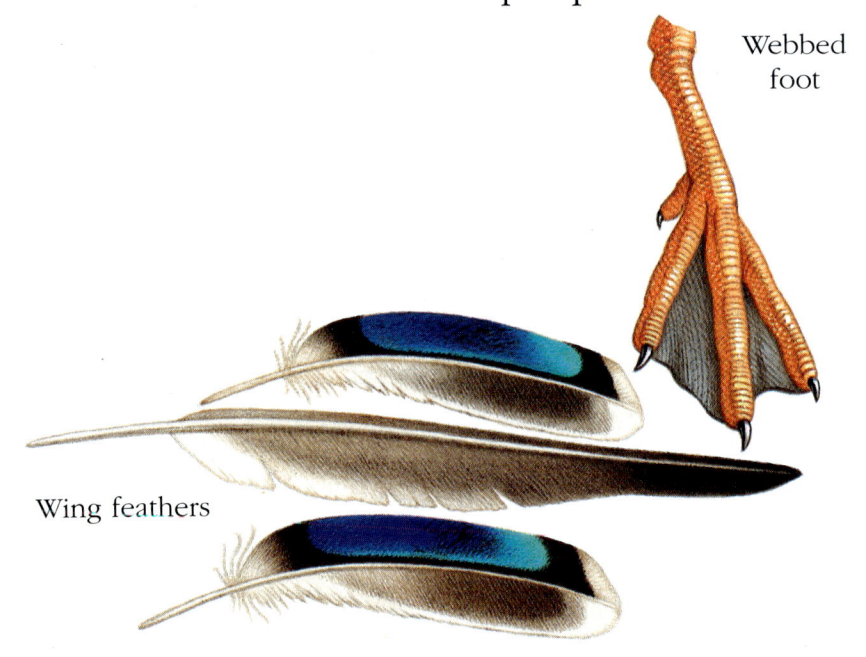

Webbed foot

Wing feathers

Ducks have webbed feet
to help them swim.
Their feathers resist water.

Different ducks have different shaped beaks, according to what they eat.

Red-breasted merganser

Shoveler

White-headed duck

Eider

The merganser has tiny 'teeth' on its beak for gripping fish. The shoveler has a flattened beak that's good for filtering water.

In spring, drakes (male ducks) parade their coloured feathers and show off to the females.

The less colourful females,
or ducks, watch the drakes.
Soon they form pairs and mate.

These eider ducks have just mated.
The female pulls soft downy feathers
from her breast. They will make
a warm lining for her nest.

Eider ducks

Female

Male

The ducklings
hatch out of the eggs
after 25-28 days.
They soon dry out.
From now on they will
follow their mother.

These mallard are dabbling ducks.
Teal, wigeon and shoveler ducks
are dabblers too. They all feed
from the surface of the water.

Dabblers tilt their tail in the air
and dip their head down
into the water.

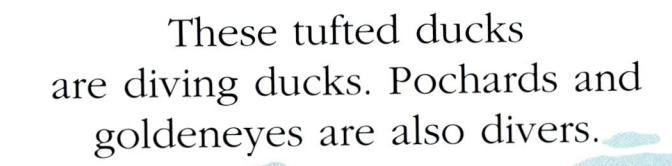

These tufted ducks
are diving ducks. Pochards and
goldeneyes are also divers.

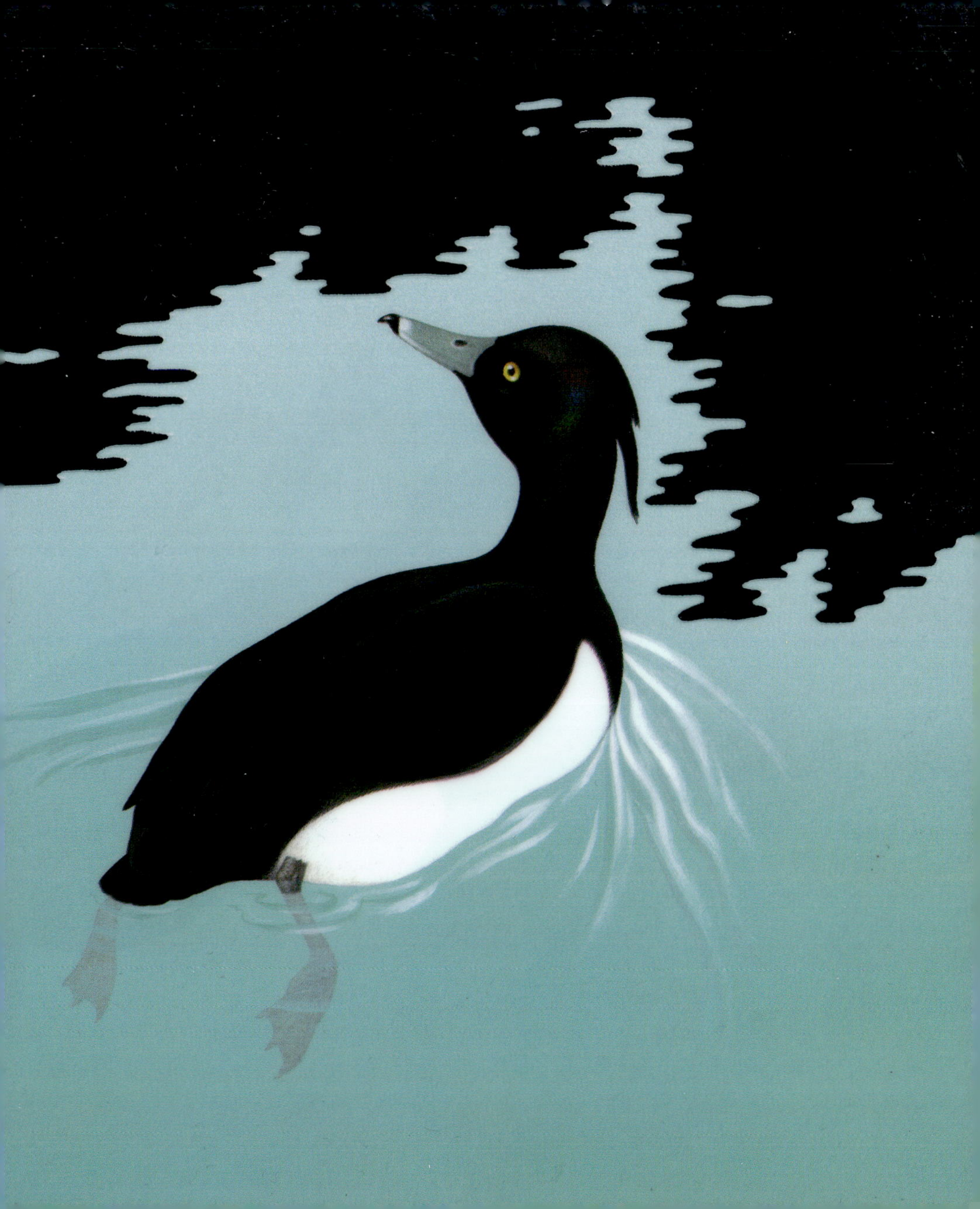

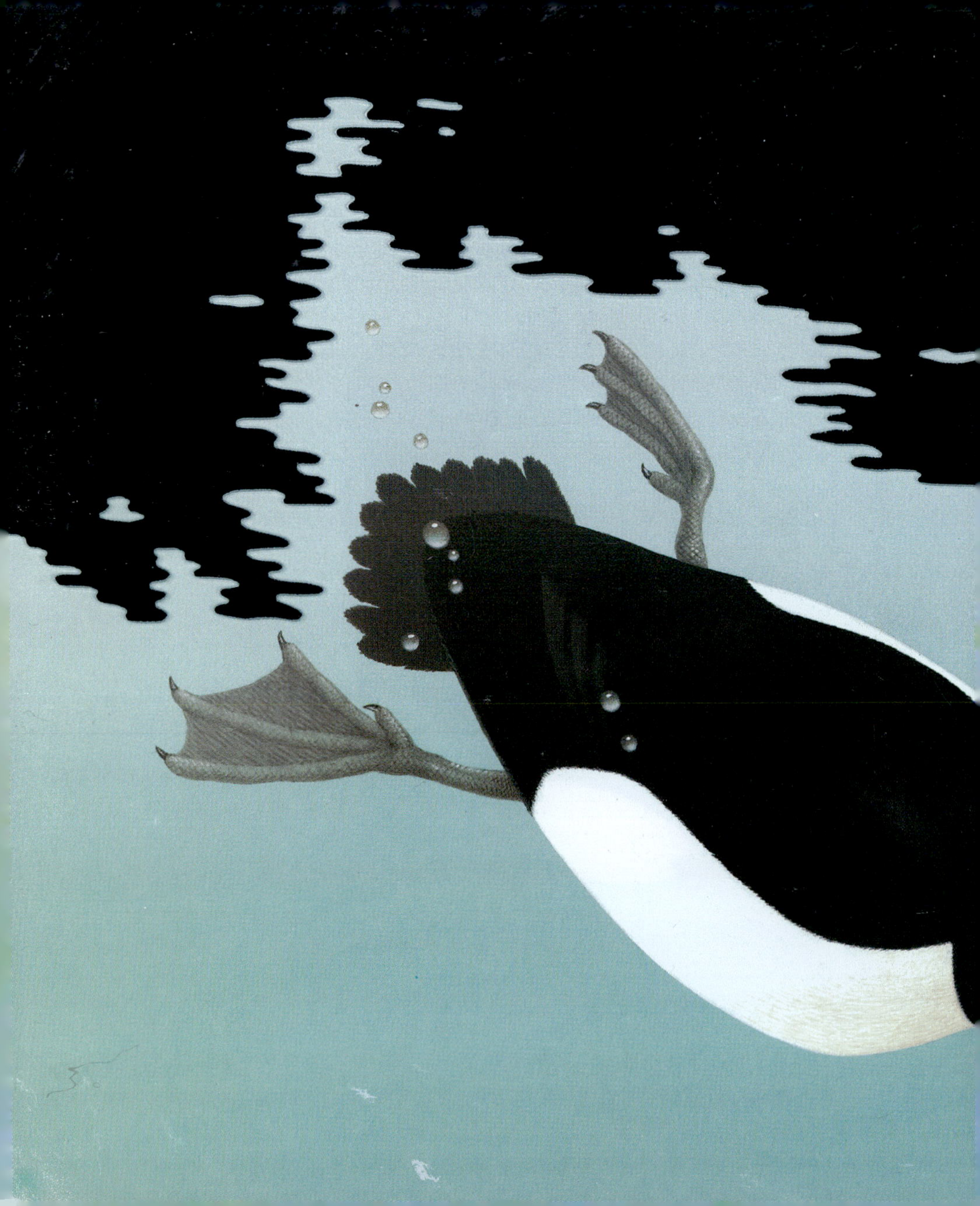

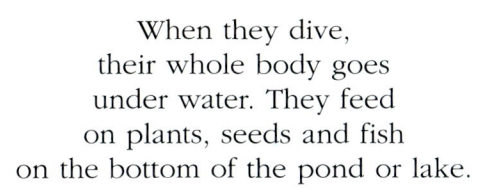

When they dive,
their whole body goes
under water. They feed
on plants, seeds and fish
on the bottom of the pond or lake.

The domestic ducks
you see on farms were bred from
mallard and other wild ducks.

Muscovy duck

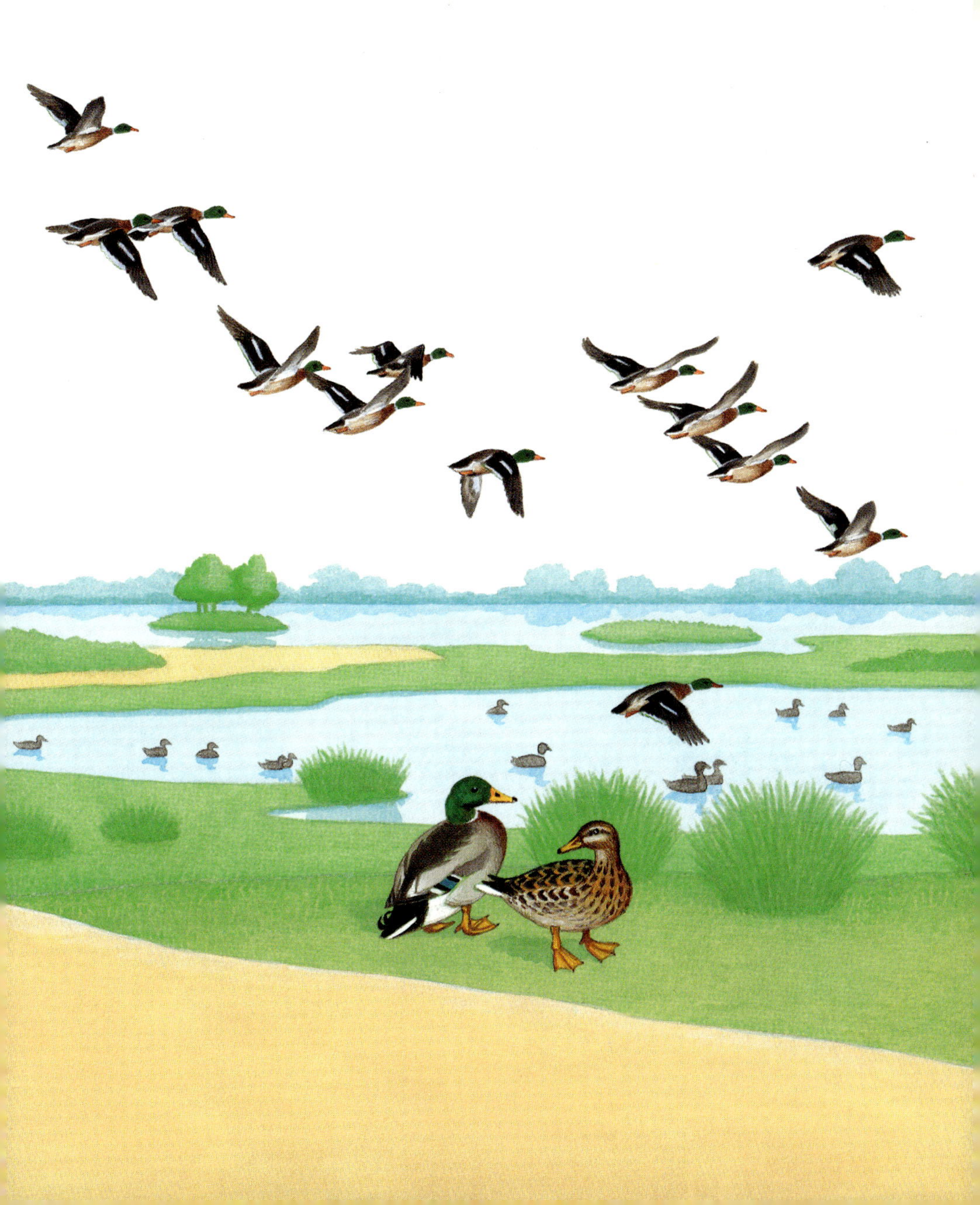

Swans, like ducks, are water birds with webbed feet.

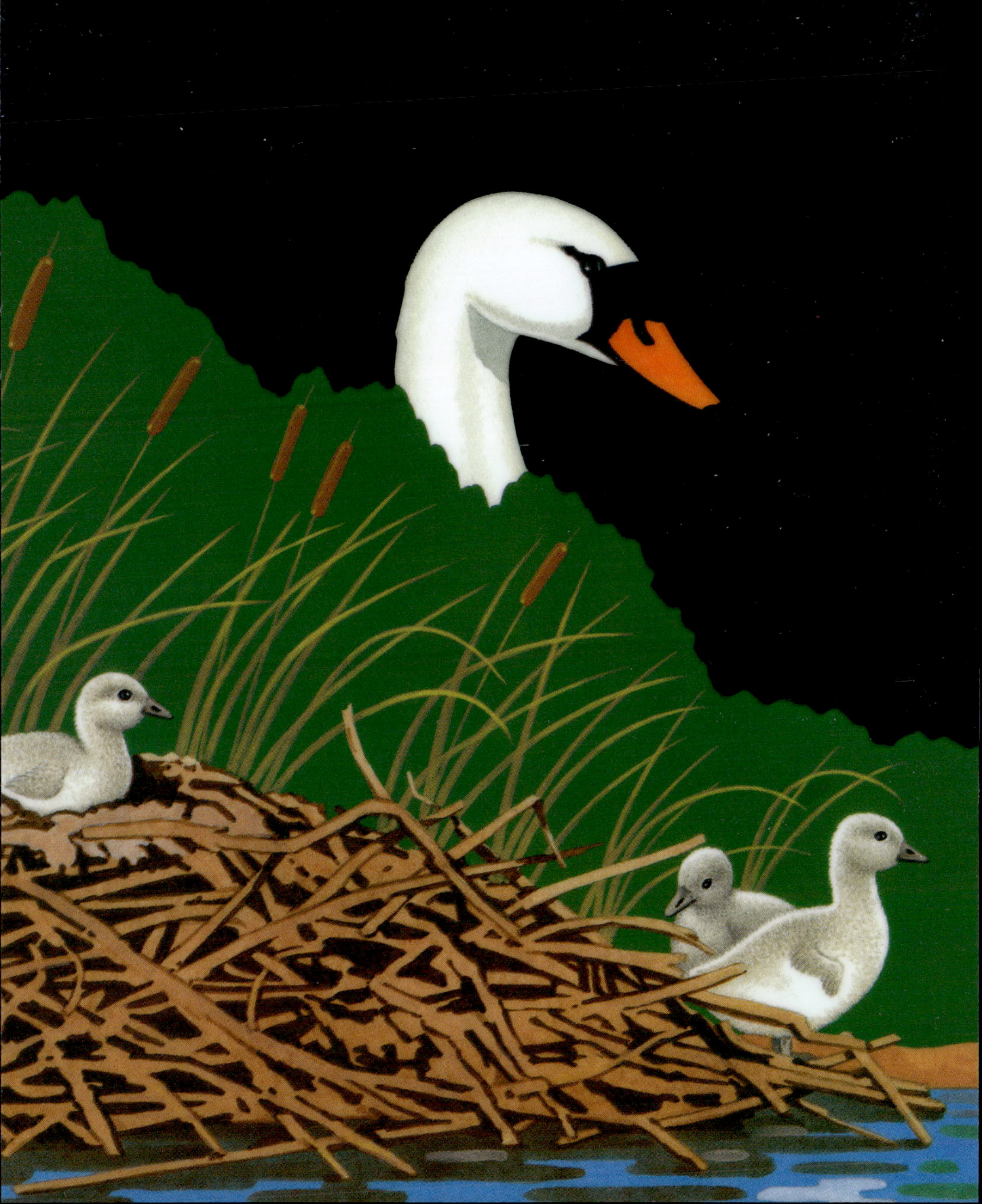

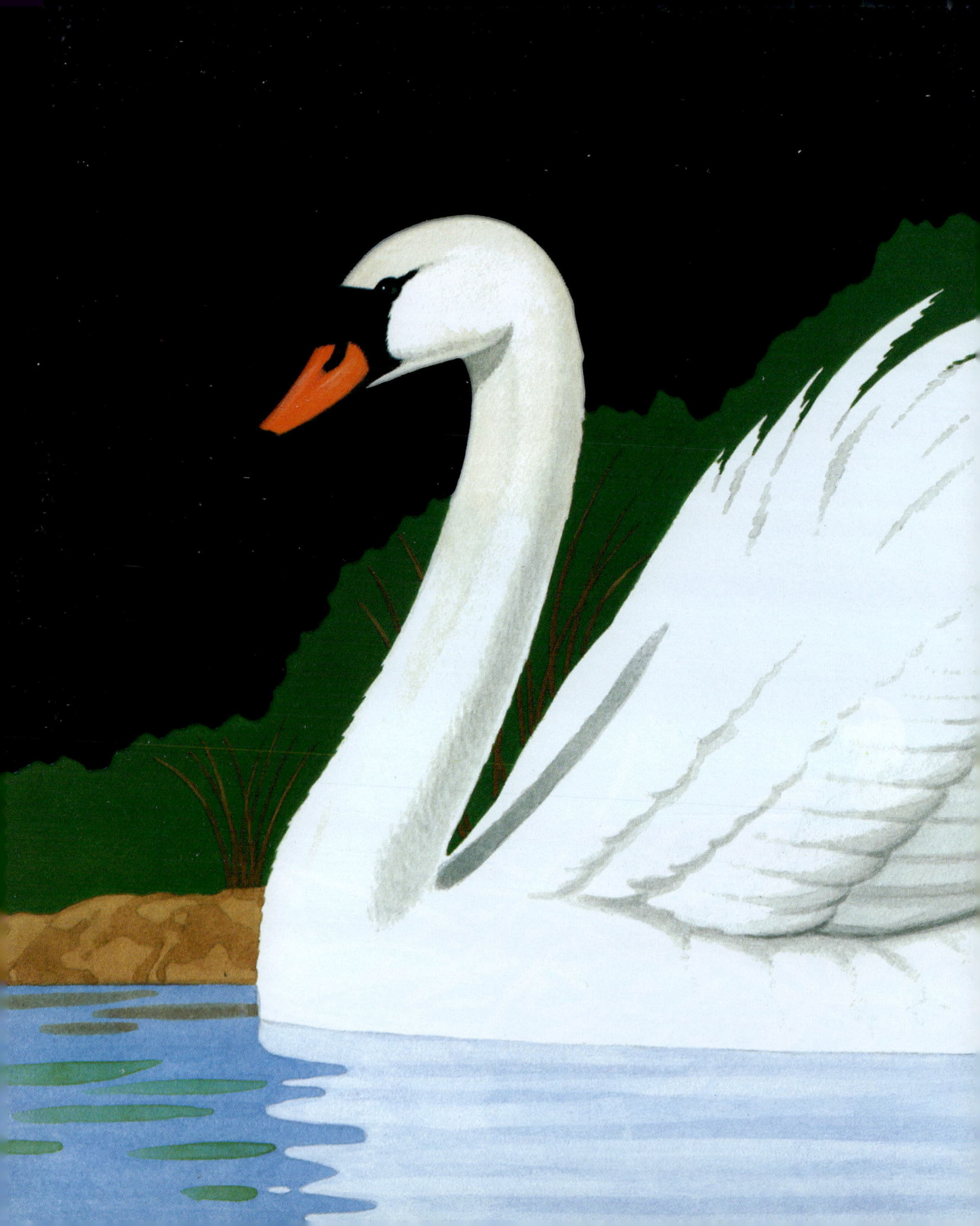

Like ducklings, cygnets follow their mother as soon as they hatch out of the egg.

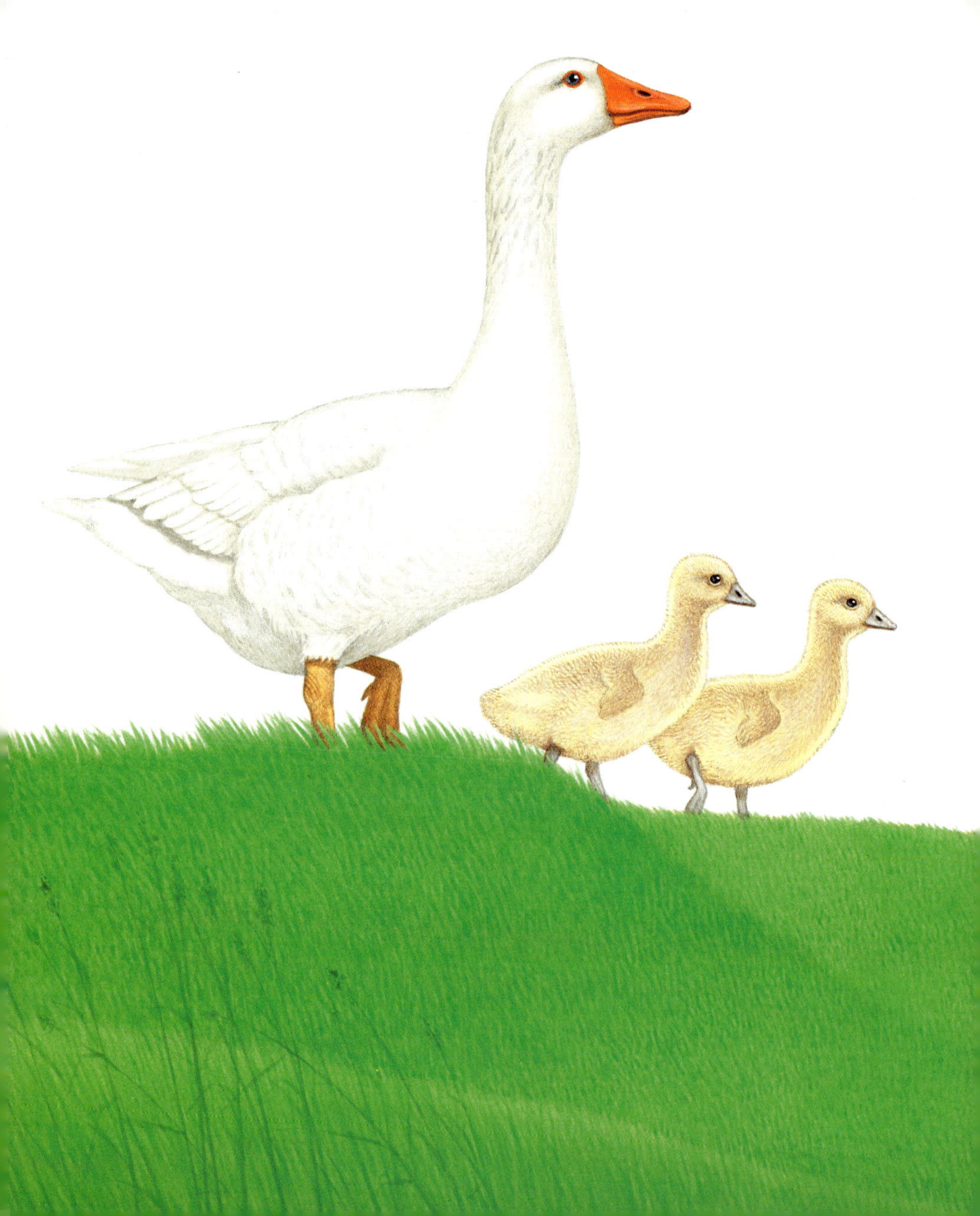

For geese, too, family bonds
are very important.

Goslings stay with their parents
for nearly a year.

Each spring, wild geese go far north,
to the tundras of Scandinavia and Siberia,
to nest and rear their young.

Each autumn,
the geese fly south again. They fly in groups,
crying to each other to help them stay together.
They winter in the warmer south.

Some European geese spend the winter
in the Netherlands, Germany and Britain,
where they are not hunted.

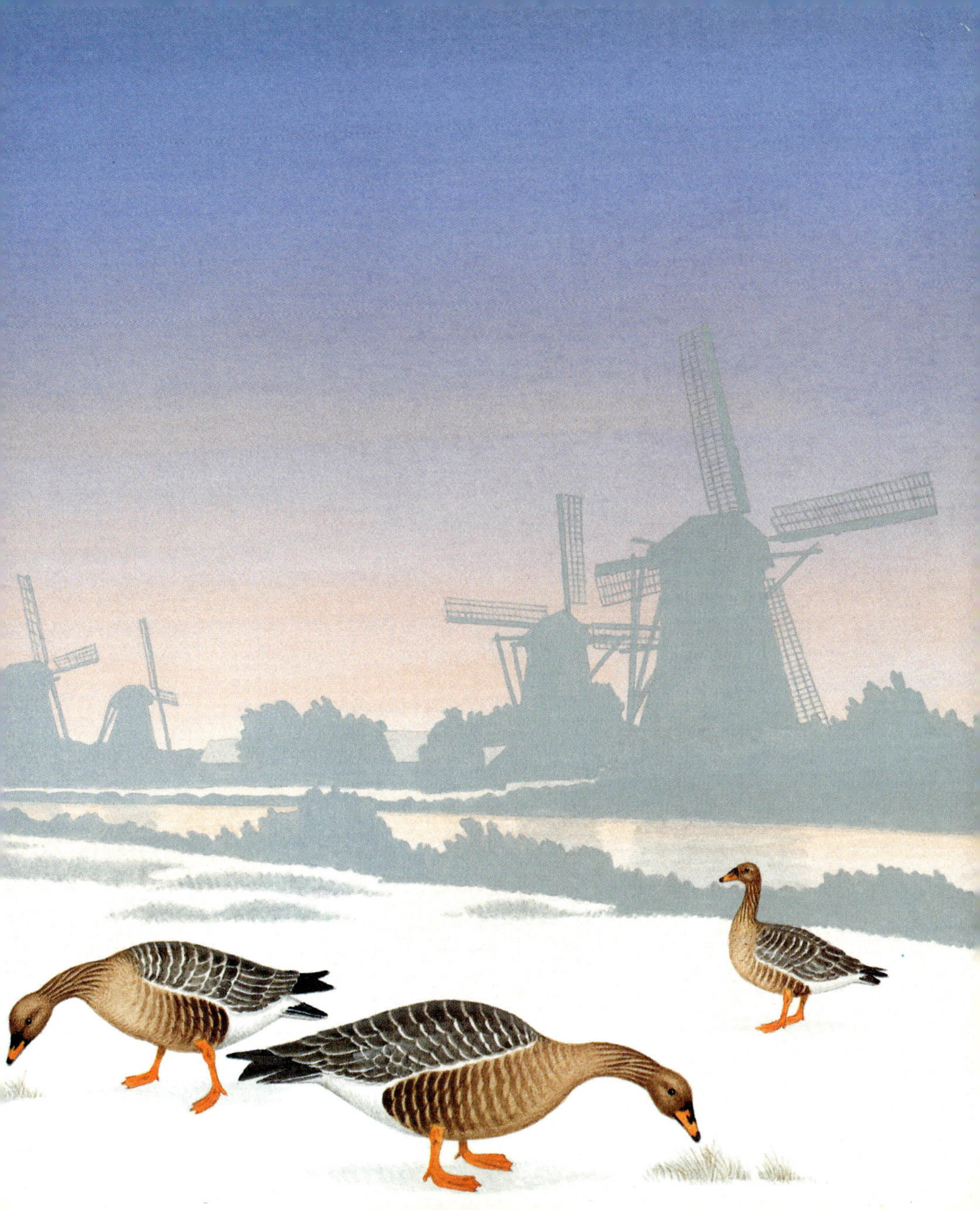

These birds all belong to the same group. They are swimmers with webbed feet.

Mandarin duck

Red-breasted goose

Canada goose

Snow goose

Baikal teal

Surf scoter

King eider

Shelduck

Harlequin

FIRST DISCOVERY
NOW THERE ARE 90 TITLES AVAILABLE IN SIX SERIES:

ABOUT ANIMALS
The Egg
Birds
The Owl
The Eagle
Ducks
Penguins
Farm Animals
The Elephant
Whales
The Horse
Monkeys & Apes
The Beaver
Bears
The Wolf
Dogs
Cats
The Mouse
Small Animals in our Homes
The Ladybird
The Bee
The Butterfly
The Frog
Dinosaurs

ABOUT NATURE
Flowers
Fruit
Vegetables
The Tree
Water
The Riverbank
Under the Ground
The Jungle
Earth and Sky
The Seashore
Weather

ABOUT PEOPLE
Colours
Counting
Up & Down
Time
Light
Pictures
Shapes
Music
Christmas and New Year
Prehistoric People
Pyramids
Homes
The Building Site
The Town
The Castle
Cathedrals
Clothes and Costumes
American Indians
Flying
On Wheels
Boats
Trains
Sport
Football
Fire-Fighting
The Toolbox
The Telephone
The Story of Bread
Shops
Hands, Feet and Paws
Babies
The Body
How the Body Works

FIRST DISCOVERY / ATLAS
Animal Atlas
Plant Atlas
Atlas of Countries
Atlas of Peoples
Atlas of Animals in Danger
Atlas of Space
Atlas of the Earth
Atlas of Civilisations
Atlas of Islands
Atlas of France

FIRST DISCOVERY / ART
Portraits
Landscapes
Animals
Paintings
Let's Visit the Louvre
Sculpture
Vincent van Gogh
Henri Matisse
Pablo Picasso

FIRST DISCOVERY / TORCHLIGHT
Let's Look at Dinosaurs
Let's Look at Insects
Let's Look at Animals Underground
Let's Look at Animals by Night

Translator: Clare Best
Editorial adviser: Sarah Heath
ISBN 1 85103 278 9
© 1997 by Editions Gallimard
English text © 1998 by Moonlight Publishing Ltd
First published in the United Kingdom 1998
by Moonlight Publishing Ltd, 36 Stratford Road, London W8
Printed in Italy by Editoriale Libraria